FROM FEAR TO FAITH

FROM FEAR TO FAITH

by

D. MARTYN LLOYD-JONES

INTER-VARSITY PRESS

Inter-Varsity Press
38 De Montfort Street, Leicester LE1 7GP, England

© D MARTYN LLOYD-JONES 1953

First Edition 1953
Reprinted 1955, 1957, 1959, 1961, 1963 1964
Reprinted in this format 1966, 1967, 1970, 1972, 1973,
1976, 1979, 1983

ISBN 0-85110-332-4

Printed in Great Britain by J. W. Arrowsmith Ltd.,
Winterstoke Road, Bristol

Inter-Varsity Press is the publishing division of the
Universities and Colleges Christian Fellowship
(formerly the Inter-Varsity Fellowship), a student
movement linking Christian Unions in universities and
colleges throughout the British Isles, and a member
movement of the International Fellowship of Evangelical
Students. For information about local and national
activities in Great Britain write to UCCF, 38 De Montfort
Street, Leicester LE1 7GP.

CONTENTS

THE MYSTERY OF HISTORICAL PROCESSES

THERE are many and varied problems in connection with the life of faith. We are never
promised in the Bible that our lives as Christian
people in this world will be free from difficulty and
trial. There is an adversary of our souls who is ever
active. His great object is always to discourage us, and
if possible to get us even to deny the faith. Various
temptations are presented by him to our minds—anything, indeed, that may undermine our faith.

Now one of the main anxieties in the realm of faith
today is what we may call ' the problem of history '.
It is about the historical situation that so many people
now seem to be perplexed. This has not always been
the case. Towards the end of the last century, and
perhaps until 1914, the main difficulty confronting
those who belonged to the faith was not ' the problem
of history ', but ' the problem of science '. In that
period, the attack upon the faith claimed the authority
of scientists and their discoveries. The difficulty then
seemed to be one of reconciling the teaching of the Bible
with the observed facts in nature and the various claims
of science.

It is true, of course, that there are still people who
are troubled in the same way; but this is not now the
main problem. The old conflict between science and
religion is really out of date. Scientists themselves have
put it out of date by rejecting, for the most part, the
materialistic and mechanical notions which governed

the popular scientific mind up to twenty years ago. In the realm of physics, recent discoveries and theories have put an end to such notions, and we have witnessed in our own time more than one outstanding scientist having to confess that he has been driven to believe in a Mind behind the universe.

It is not the scientific problem, therefore, but the mystery of history which gives anxiety now. That is the problem of problems in this twentieth century. It naturally arises from the events of this period. Our fathers, and to an even greater degree our grandfathers, were not particularly concerned with the problem of history because life was moving in leisurely fashion and, as they believed, inevitably towards a wonderful goal of perfection. The Promised Land was about to be occupied. They just had to go on quietly and they would soon be there. But we in this century have all been shaken to our foundations by the course of events and, in face of these things, many have found their faith sorely tried. They have found it difficult, for example, to account for two devastating world wars, for such events seem incompatible with the biblical teaching concerning the providence of God.

Now it must be stated at once that this is a problem which should never have led anyone to feel unhappy or perplexed. There is really no excuse for this because of the plain teaching of the Bible itself. From one point of view there was never any excuse, either, for being in perplexity about science and religion. But there is still less excuse for anyone to be in trouble over this problem of history, because the Bible deals with it in the clearest possible manner. Why then are people troubled about it?

The main reason, it would seem, is that there are those who use the Bible in a narrow sense, as being exclusively a text book of personal salvation. Many people seem to think that the sole theme of the Bible is that of man's personal relationship to God. Of course that is one of the central themes, and we thank God for the salvation provided without which we should be left in hopeless despair. But that is not the only theme of the Bible. Indeed, we can go so far as to say that the Bible puts the question of personal salvation into a larger context. Ultimately the main message of the Bible concerns the condition of the entire world and its destiny; and you and I, as individuals, are a part of that larger whole. That is why it starts with the creation of the world rather than of man. The trouble is that we are inclined to be exclusively concerned with our own personal problem, whereas the Bible starts further back: it puts every problem in the context of this world view.

If we do not realize that the Bible has a particular world view, it is not surprising that the world in its present state makes us despair. But if we read right through the Bible and note its message, instead of just picking out an occasional Psalm, or the Sermon on the Mount, or our favourite Gospel, we shall find it has a profound philosophy of history, and a distinctive world view. It enables us to understand what is happening today and that nothing that occurs in history fails to find a place in the divine programme. The great and noble teaching of the Bible is concerned with the whole question of the world and its destiny.

In the book of the prophet Habakkuk we have a perfect illustration of this. The prophet treats the problem of history in a particularly interesting manner; not as an academic or theoretical philosophy of history, but as the personal perplexity of one man—the prophet himself. He wrote his book to relate his own experience.

Here was a man greatly troubled by what was happening. He was anxious to reconcile what he saw with what he believed. The same approach to the question is found elsewhere in the Bible, particularly in the Psalms,[1] and every one of the prophets deals with this same problem of history. But not only are the books of the Old Testament occupied with this problem; the attentive reader will find it running right through the New Testament as well. He will find our Lord giving His pre-view of history, and in the book of Revelation he will meet another fore-view of history and of the relationship of our risen Lord and the Christian Church to that history. We should awake to the fact that ' the problem of history ' is the great theme of Holy Scripture.

In approaching the study of the book of Habakkuk we may first of all consider the situation confronting the prophet personally. Then we can proceed to deduce certain principles. Thus we shall see that, in essence, everything that caused anxiety to the prophet is exactly what is worrying so many people today as they try to relate all they observe to the teaching of Scripture, especially to the teaching about the being and character of God.

The prophet saw Israel in a very backslidden condition. She had turned away from God and forgotten Him. She had given herself over to false gods and other unworthy pursuits. No wonder that he exclaims in acute distress of mind: ' O Lord, how long shall I cry, and thou wilt not hear! even cry out unto thee of violence, and thou wilt not save! Why dost thou shew me iniquity (and he is thinking of his own nation and people) and cause me to behold grievance? for spoiling and violence are before me: and there are (those) that

[1] One of the classical statements is to be found in Psalm lxxiii.

raise up strife and contention. Therefore the law is slacked, and judgment doth never go forth: for the wicked doth compass about the righteous; therefore wrong judgment proceedeth.'

What a terrible picture! Sin, immorality and vice were rampant, while those who were in authority and entrusted with government were slack and indolent. They did not apply the law equitably and honestly. There was lawlessness everywhere; and whenever anyone ventured to remonstrate with the people as the prophet did, those in authority rose up with strife and contention. Serious religious falling away had been followed, as invariably happens, by a general moral and political decline. Such were the alarming conditions which confronted the prophet.

It was a real problem. To start with, he could not understand why God allowed it all. He had been praying to God about it, but God did not seem to answer. Hence his perplexity: 'O Lord, how long shall I cry, and thou wilt not hear! even cry out unto thee of violence, and thou wilt not save!' But, unfortunately for the prophet, this was only the beginning of his troubles. For following his complaint that God had failed to listen to him and to answer his prayers, God did answer him, but in an altogether unexpected way. 'Behold ye among the heathen, and regard, and wonder marvellously: for I will work a work in your days, which ye will not believe, though it be told you. For, lo, I raise up the Chaldeans, that bitter and hasty nation, which shall march through the breadth of the land, to possess the dwellingplaces that are not theirs.' God was virtually saying to the prophet, 'All right! I have been hearing your prayer all the time, and now I tell you what I propose to do. I am going to raise up the Chaldeans.' The Chaldeans were, at that time, a very insignificant people compared with the Assyrians, who were the great contemporaries of Israel. Habakkuk, already perplexed at the fact that God permitted iniquity in His own nation, is now told that God intends to raise up an utterly pagan, godless people to conquer the land and to punish His people. The prophet was almost overwhelmed. This is the problem which we shall study in the following chapters.

OUTLINE
OF THE BOOK OF HABAKKUK

In i. 5–11 God tells the prophet what He is about to do. He reveals the might of Israel's terrible enemy and the devastation which he will leave behind him. He describes the enemy's arrogance and pride in imputing his success to his own god and to his own greatness. In i. 12—ii. 1 we see the way in which the prophet grapples with this problem. The rest of chapter ii is devoted to God's gracious dealings with Habakkuk, and the way in which He enables him to understand the over-all situation. God gives him a wonderful insight into biblical philosophy and history, and how these things are to be reconciled with His own holiness and greatness, and how everything will eventually be perfectly worked out. Chapter iii describes the prophet's reaction to all this.

CHAPTER ONE

THE STRANGENESS OF GOD'S WAYS

Habakkuk i. 1–11

THE message of Habakkuk is sorely needed in these days when so many are perplexed by this problem of history. We begin, therefore, with two statements of fact:

I. GOD'S WAYS ARE OFTEN MYSTERIOUS

(a) *His inaction*

The first thing we discover when we study God's actions is *that He may seem to be strangely silent and inactive in provocative circumstances.* Why is it that God permits certain things to happen? Why is the Christian Church what she is today? Look at her history over the last forty or fifty years. Why has God permitted such conditions? Why has He allowed ' modernism ' to arise, undermining the faith and even denying its fundamental truths? Why does He not strike these people dead as they utter their blasphemy and their denials of the faith which they are ordained to preach? Why does He allow so many wrong things to be done *even in His name*?

Again, why has not God answered the prayers of His faithful people? We have been praying for revival for thirty or forty years. Our prayers have been sincere and zealous. We have bemoaned the state of affairs and have cried out to God on account of it. But still nothing seems to happen. Like the prophet Habakkuk many are asking ' How long shall I cry, and thou wilt not hear, even cry out unto thee of violence and thou wilt not save ? ' But this is not only the problem of the Church as a whole; it is also the question which confronts so many people personally. There are those who have been praying about someone who is dear to them for many years, and God does not seem to answer. They reason within themselves like this : ' Surely it is the will of God that a man should become a Christian ? Well, I have been praying for him for all these years and nothing seems to happen. Why? Why is God thus silent ? ' People are often impatient about this. Why does He not answer our prayers? How can we understand a holy God permitting His own Church to be as she is today ?

(b) *His unexpected providences*

A second thing we discover is *that God sometimes gives unexpected answers to our prayers*. This, more than anything else, was what really startled Habakkuk. For a long time God does not seem to answer at all. Then, when He does answer, what He says is even more mysterious than His apparent failure to listen to our prayers. Habakkuk was quite clear in his own mind that the need was for God to chastise the nation and then send a great revival. But when God replied, ' I am answering you by raising up the Chaldean army to go right through and destroy your cities ', that was the last thing he could ever have imagined that God would say. But that is what God did tell him, and that is what actually took place.

John Newton wrote a poem describing a similar personal experience. He felt that he wanted something better in his spiritual life. He cried out for a deeper knowledge of God. He expected some wonderful vision of Him rending the heavens and coming down to shower blessing into his life. But instead of this Newton had an experience in which for months God seemed to have abandoned him to Satan. He was tempted and tried beyond his comprehension. Yet at last he *did* come to understand and saw that that was God's way of answering his prayer. God had allowed him to go down into the depths to teach him to depend entirely on Him. Then, when Newton had learned his lesson, He brought him out of his trial.

We all tend to prescribe the answers to our prayers. We think that God can come in only one way. But Scripture teaches us that God sometimes answers our prayers by allowing things to become much worse before they become better. He may sometimes do the opposite of what we anticipate. He may overwhelm us by confronting us with a Chaldean army. Yet it is a fundamental principle in the life and walk of faith that we must always be prepared for the unexpected when we are dealing with God. I wonder what our fathers would have thought forty years ago if they could have had a pre-view of the state of the Christian Church today. They were unhappy enough about things even then. They were already having meetings for revival and for seeking God. If they could see the Church at the present time, they would not believe their eyes. They could never have imagined that spiritually the Church could have sunk so low. Yet God has allowed this to happen. It has been an unexpected answer. We must hold on to the hope that He has allowed things to become worse before they finally become better.

(c) His unusual instruments

A third surprising feature of God's ways is *that He sometimes uses strange instruments to correct His Church and people.* The Chaldeans, of all people, are the ones whom God is going to raise up to chastise Israel! Such a thing was unthinkable. But here again is a fact which is evident right through Scripture. God, if He so wishes, can use even a godless Chaldean. In the course of history He has used all sorts of strange and unexpected instruments to bring His purposes to pass. This is a very relevant fact today, for it would seem that, according to the Bible, much of what is happening in the world now must be regarded in this light. We may perhaps go further and say positively that Communism, which seems to be feared by so many Christians today, is but an instrument which God is using to deal with His own people.

The importance of all this lies in the fact that, if we do not view these things in the right way, our prayers will be wrongly conceived and wrongly directed. We have to realize the true state of the Church, and recognize its iniquity. We must understand that it is possible that the forces which today are most antagonistic to the Christian Church are possibly being used by God for His own purpose. The plain teaching of the prophet is that God may use very strange instruments indeed, and sometimes the very last instrument that we would have expected.

II. GOD'S WAYS ARE OFTEN MISUNDERSTOOD

(a) By careless religious people

God's ways are often strange and perplexing and surprise at what He does is felt by more than one type of person. It is, first of all, a matter of great surprise to the more careless amongst religious people. In Hab. i. 5, God refers to the godless in Israel, those who had become careless and slack. ' Behold ye among the heathen, and regard, and wonder marvellously; for I will work a work in your days, which ye will not believe, though it be told you.' Their attitude was: ' Here is that prophet telling us that God is going to use the Chaldeans. As if God could do anything like that! There is no real danger; don't listen to him. These prophets are always alarmists, and threatening us with evil. The very idea that God would raise up a people like the Chaldeans to chastise Israel! The whole thing is impossible! ' The trouble with Israel was that they would never believe the prophets. Yet, in fact, God did deal with His people exactly as He said He would.

The attitude we find in Israel is as old as the Flood. God warned the ancient world of judgment through Noah, saying, ' My Spirit shall not always strive with man '. But men scoffed and said that such a thing was monstrous and could not happen. It was the same with Sodom and Gomorrah. Easy-going people could never believe that their cities would be destroyed. They said God would intervene before that happened, and continued in their indolent ways in the hope that God would deliver them without much trouble to themselves. In the time of Habakkuk the attitude was the same. But God *did* raise up the Chaldeans, and Israel was attacked and conquered. The nation was laid low and carried away into captivity.

The most signal illustration of this principle is recorded in Acts xiii where the apostle Paul quotes the fifth verse of Habakkuk i and applies it to his contemporaries. He declares in effect: ' No, you will not believe, any more than your fathers did. But because

Israel has not recognized her Messiah, has even crucified Him, and now refuses to believe His gospel, God is at last going to act in judgment. He is going to raise up the Roman power to sack and to destroy your temple, and you yourselves will be cast out among the nations. I know you will not believe this, for the prophet Habakkuk has already prophesied it, and you are continuing to ignore his message.' The year A.D. 70 inexorably came. The Roman legions surrounded Jerusalem and destroyed it and the Jews were cast out among the nations where they remain until this day. It is true that careless religious people never believe the prophets. They always say, ' God will never do such things! ' But I am reminding you that God does so act. God may be using Communism in our time to chastise His own people and to teach them a lesson. We dare not continue, therefore, to be smug and indolent, saying it is unthinkable that God could use such an instrument. We must not allow ourselves to be lulled into the state of those who dwell at ease in Zion and who fail to read the signs of the times.

(b) By the world

In the second place, God's ways are very surprising to the world. ' Then shall his mind change, and he shall pass over, and offend, imputing this his power unto his god ' (Hab. i. 11). The Chaldeans completely failed to realize that they were being used by God and imputed all their success to their own god. They thought that they owed their success to their own military prowess, and boasted of the fact. But God was soon to demonstrate to them that it was not so, and that as He had raised them up so He could cast them down. The world, even more than God's own people, fails to understand God's ways. Those arrogant

powers, which have been used by God for His own
purpose at various times in history, have always prided
themselves on their achievements. The pride of the
modern world in its scientific progress and in its
political systems is typical of this. Because the enemies
of the Christian faith see the Church languishing and
find themselves coming into the ascendancy, they
impute their success ' unto their own God '. They fail
to understand the true meaning of history. Great
powers have been raised up and have conquered for a
while, but they have always become drunk with their
own successes. And suddenly, they in turn have found
themselves cast down. The real significance of history
never dawns upon them.

(c) *By the prophet himself*

Lastly, God's ways were baffling even to the prophet
himself. But his reaction was a very different one.
His question was as to how all this is to be reconciled
with the holiness of God. He exclaims, ' O Lord, how
long shall I cry, and thou wilt not hear! even cry out
unto thee of violence, and thou wilt not save! Why
dost thou shew me iniquity, and cause me to behold
grievance? for spoiling and violence are before me:
and there are (those) that raise up strife and contention.'

★   ★   ★

It must suffice to establish the following general biblical
principles by way of an answer to this problem of
history:

I. HISTORY IS UNDER DIVINE CONTROL

' For, lo, I raise up the Chaldeans, that bitter and
hasty nation.' God controls not only Israel, but also

His enemies, the Chaldeans. Every nation on earth is
under the hand of God, for there is no power in this
world that is not ultimately controlled by Him. Things
are not what they appear to be. It seemed to be the
astute military prowess of the Chaldeans that had
brought them into the ascendancy. But it was not so
at all, for God had raised them up. God is the Lord of
history. He is seated in the heavens and the nations
to Him are ' as grasshoppers, as a drop in a bucket, or
as the small dust of the balance'. The Bible asserts that
God is over all. He started the historical process, He
is controlling it, and He is going to end it. We must
never lose sight of this crucial fact.

II. HISTORY FOLLOWS A DIVINE PLAN

Things do not just happen. Events are not just
accidental, for there is a definite plan of history and
everything has been pre-arranged from the beginning.
God who ' sees the end from the beginning' has a
purpose in it all, and knows ' the times and the seasons '.
He knows when to bless Israel and when not to bless
her. Everything is under His hand. It was ' when the
fullness of the time was come' that God sent forth His
Son. He allowed the great philosophers, with their
clarification of thought, to come first. Then emerged
the Romans, famous for ordered government, building
their roads and spreading their wonderful legal system
throughout the world. It was after this that God sent
forth His Son. God had planned it all.

There is a purpose in history, and what is now
happening in this twentieth century is not accidental.
Remembering that the Church is at the centre of God's
plan, let us never forget the pride and arrogance of the
Church in the nineteenth century. Behold her sitting

back in self-satisfaction, enjoying her so-called cultured sermons and learned ministry, feeling just a little ashamed to mention such things as conversion and the work of the Holy Spirit. Observe the prosperous Victorian comfortably enjoying his worship. Note his faith in science and his readiness to substitute philosophy for revelation. How constantly he denied the very spirit of the New Testament! Yes, the Church needed chastisement, and it is not at all difficult to understand this twentieth century when we consider the story of the nineteenth. There is indeed a plan discernible in all these things.

III. HISTORY FOLLOWS A DIVINE TIMETABLE

God does not stop to consult us, and everything takes place according to ' the counsel of His own will '. God has His time; He has His own way; and He acts and works accordingly.

IV. HISTORY IS BOUND UP WITH THE DIVINE KINGDOM

The key to the history of the world is the kingdom of God. The story of the other nations mentioned in the Old Testament is relevant only as it bears upon the destiny of Israel. And ultimately history today is relevant only as it bears upon the history of the Christian Church. What really matters in the world is God's kingdom. From the very beginning, since the fall of man, God has been at work establishing a new kingdom in the world. It is His own kingdom, and He is calling people out of the world into that kingdom; and everything that happens in the world has relevance to it. It is still only in process of formation, but it will finally reach its perfect consummation. Other events are of importance as they have a bearing upon that event.

The problems of today are to be understood only in its light. What God is permitting in the Church and in the world today is related to His great purpose for His own Church and kingdom.

Let us not therefore be stumbled when we see surprising things happening in the world. Rather let us ask, ' What is the relevance of this event to the kingdom of God? ' Or, if strange things are happening to you personally, don't complain, but say, ' What is God teaching me through this? What is there in me that needs to be corrected? Where have I gone wrong and why is God allowing these things ? ' There is a meaning in them if only we can see it. We need not become bewildered and doubt the love or the justice of God. If God were unkind enough to answer some of our prayers at once, and in our way, we should be very impoverished Christians. Fortunately, God sometimes delays His answer in order to deal with selfishness or things in our lives which should not be there. He is concerned about us, and intends to fit us for a fuller place in His kingdom. We should therefore judge every event in the light of God's great, eternal and glorious purpose.

CHAPTER TWO

THE PROPHET'S PERPLEXITY

Habakkuk i. 12–17
(especially verses 12 and 13)

IT is important for the Christian not only to read the newspapers and to understand something of what is happening in the world, but to understand the significance of events. There are, in our time, grave dangers confronting the Church and, unless she is careful, like Israel of old she may enter into political alliances to try to stave off the very thing which God has ordained. It is essential that the Church should not view things with a political eye, but learn to interpret events spiritually and to understand them in the light of God's instructions to her. What to the natural man is utterly abhorrent, and even disastrous, may be the very thing God is using to chastise us and to restore us to a right relationship to Himself. So we must not jump to hasty conclusions.

I. THE IMPORTANCE OF RIGHT METHODS OF APPROACH

Most of the problems and perplexities of the Christian life arise from a lack of the right *method* of approach. It is much more important that we should know the method of approach than that we should have pat answers to particular problems. People usually want a clear answer to a specific question, but the Bible does not always give us what we desire in this respect. It does, however, teach us a method. We are apt to panic and to jump to false conclusions when the unexpected happens and when God is dealing with us in a strange and unusual manner. In Psalm lxxiii we are taught the danger of speaking unadvisedly with our lips. The Psalmist, seeing certain evils, exclaimed, ' Verily I have cleansed my heart in vain, and washed my hands in innocency.' Was there any point, therefore, in being religious? But he suddenly pulled himself up and said, ' If I should speak thus . . . ,' realizing that he had spoken unadvisedly with his lips. He had begun to speak without really thinking.

In every such situation we must discover the right way to act. The problem may come in a personal form; it may come to us nationally; or it may come to us as world citizens in the wider sphere of historical events. So let us analyze carefully this perfect example of the method of approach of which so many are found in the Bible.

II. THE METHOD DESCRIBED

(a) Stop to think

The first rule is to think instead of speaking. ' Be swift to hear,' says James, ' slow to speak, slow to wrath ' (Jas. i. 19). Our trouble is that we are swift to speak and swift to wrath, but slow to think. According to this prophet, however, the first thing to do is to ponder. Before expressing our reactions we must discipline ourselves to think. It may seem superfluous to emphasize this, yet we all know well that this is where we most often go wrong.

(b) Re-state basic principles

The next rule is that when you start to think you must not begin with your immediate problem. Begin further back. Apply the strategy of the indirect approach. This is a well-known principle in military planning. The real enemy in the last war was Germany, but the Allies began to defeat Germany in North Africa, a strategy of indirect approach. Such an approach is sometimes of vital importance in the spiritual life, especially when we are confronted with a problem such as the one before us. We need to start our thinking further back, and to approach the immediate problem indirectly.

We must first remind ourselves of those things of which we are absolutely certain, things which are entirely beyond doubt. Write them down and say to yourself: ' In this terrible and perplexing situation in which I find myself, here at least is solid ground.' When, walking on moorlands, or over a mountain range, you come to bogs, the only way to negotiate them is to find solid places on which you can place your feet. The way to get across the morasses and the places in which you are liable to sink is to search for footholds. So, in spiritual problems, you must return to eternal and absolute principles. The psychology of this is obvious, for the moment you turn to basic principles, you immediately begin to lose your sense of panic. It is a great thing to reassure your soul with those things that are beyond dispute.

(c) *Apply the principles to the problem*

Then, having done that, you can take the next step. Put the particular problem into the context of those firm principles which are before you. The fact of the matter is that all problems are capable of solution only if they are put into the right context. The way to interpret a difficult text of Scripture is to consider its context. We often mistake the meaning of a phrase because we take it out of its context; but when you put your problem text into its context, the context will generally interpret the text for you. The same is also true of the particular problem that is causing you concern.

(d) If still in doubt, commit the problem to God in faith

That brings us to the final step in this method. If you are *still* not clear about the answer, then just take it to God in prayer and leave it there with Him. That is what the prophet did in i. 13. In the preceding verse and in the early part of verse 13, the prophet was clearly still perplexed, so he took the problem to God and left it there.

Once we have the right method we can apply it to any problem: to God's strange dealings with a nation, to problems in the world, or equally to personal difficulties. Whatever the problem, stop to think, lay down the propositions, bring it into that context, and then, if still in trouble, take it to God and leave it there.

★　　　★　　　★

Let us follow the prophet as he applies this method to the two major problems that troubled him, that of the apparent weakness and defeat of God, and that of reconciling God's use of the Chaldean army with His holy character.

I. THE PROBLEM OF GOD'S INACTION

People were then asking: Why did God allow the Chaldean army to behave as it liked and with such devastating results? Was He helpless in face of that enemy power? People are still asking: Why did God allow the ' higher critics ' and other debilitating influences to come in? Why does He tolerate such things?

Why doesn't He intervene ? Is it because He cannot stop it? Or again, Why does God allow war?

(a) God is eternal

After stating his difficulty the prophet declares, ' Art thou not from everlasting?' (i. 12). You see, he is laying down a proposition. He is forgetting for a moment the immediate problem, and asking himself what it was he was sure of about God. The first thing was ' Art thou not from everlasting?' Previously he had just said (i. 11) that the Chaldeans, flushed with success, imputed their power to their god; and the moment he said that he began to think, ' Their god— what is their god? Just something they have made themselves. This Bel of theirs is of their own manufacture!' (cf. Is. xlvi). And as he thought thus, he reminded himself of something of which he was sure. God is the eternal God, the everlasting God, from everlasting to everlasting. He is not like the gods whom men worship; He is not like the god of the proud Chaldean army; He is God from eternity to eternity, the everlasting God. There is nothing more consoling or reassuring when oppressed by the problems of history, and when wondering what is to happen in the world, than to remember that the God whom we worship is outside the flux of history. He has preceded history; He has created history. His throne is above the world and outside time. He reigns in eternity, the everlasting God.

(b) God is self-existent

Then he adds something else: ' Art thou not from everlasting, O Lord,' and he uses the great name ' Jehovah '. ' Art thou not from everlasting, O Jehovah?' That name tells us that God is the self-existing

One, the eternal I AM. ' Go and tell them,' God had said to Moses, ' that I AM hath sent me unto you.' The name ' I AM that I AM ' means ' I am the Absolute, the self-existent One '. Here is a second vital proposition. God is not in any sense dependent upon anything that happens in the world, but He is self-existent within Himself. Not only is He *not* dependent upon the world, but He need never have created it had He not willed to do so. The tremendous truth concerning the Trinity is that an eternally self-existent life resides in the Godhead—Father, Son and Holy Spirit. Here again is wonderful reassurance: ' I am certain that God is not dependent upon this world but that He is self-existent; He is Lord, He is Jehovah, the great I AM.' The problem begins to fade.

(c) *God is holy*

The prophet then reminds himself that another absolute in God is His holiness. ' Art thou not from everlasting, O Lord my God, mine Holy One? ' He is sure not only of His eternal existence, not only of His self-existence, and His independence of everything and everybody, but that He is the ' Holy One ', utterly, absolutely righteous and holy, ' a consuming fire '. ' God is light and in Him is no darkness at all.' And the moment you consider Scriptures like that you are forced to ask, ' Can the Lord of the earth do that which is unrighteous? ' Such a thing is unthinkable.

(d) *God is almighty*

Then follows the prophet's next proposition. He goes on to say, ' O Lord, thou hast ordained them for judgment; and, O mighty God, thou hast established them for correction.' So another thing of which he is certain is that God is all-powerful. The word in

Hebrew translated ' mighty God ' literally means ' a
rock ', conveying the idea of the strength and the
almightiness of God. The God who created the whole
world out of nothing, who said, ' Let there be light ' and
there was light, has absolute power; He has illimitable
might. He is ' The Rock '.

(e) God is faithful

There is yet one other proposition which the prophet
lays down concerning God, which is in many ways the
most important of all with respect to the problem confronting him: ' Art thou not from everlasting, O Lord
my God, mine Holy One? we shall not die.' What is
the significance of those words: ' My God, mine Holy
One, we shall not die '? He is recalling that God is the
God of the Covenant. Though He is independent and
absolute, eternal, mighty, righteous and holy, nevertheless He has condescended to make a covenant with
men. He made a covenant with Abraham, to which
the prophet is referring here, and He renewed this
covenant with Isaac and Jacob. He renewed it again
with David. It was this covenant that entitled Israel
to turn to God and say, ' My God, mine Holy One.'
The prophet remembers that God has said, ' I will be
their God and they shall be my people.' For those
saintly men, the prophets, and all who had spiritual
understanding in Israel, this fact was more significant
than anything else. While believing in the eternal
attributes of God, they might have been chilled by the
thought that such a God might be far away in the
heavens and oblivious of their need. But what linked
Him to them was the knowledge that He was a faithful,
covenant-keeping God. God had given His word and
He would never break it. The prophet, thinking of the
covenant, is able to say, ' My God, mine Holy One ';

and so he adds ' we shall not die '. Whatever the Chaldean army might do it could never exterminate Israel, because God had given certain promises to Israel which He could never break.

Having stated his propositions, the prophet now proceeds to bring his problem into the context of those absolute and eternal principles. And this is what he says: ' Thou hast ordained them for judgment . . . thou hast established them for correction.' He reaches his answer to this question about the Chaldeans by reasoning like this: ' God must be raising them up for Israel's benefit; of this I can be absolutely certain. It is not that the Chaldeans have taken the law into their own hands; it is not that God is incapable of restraining them. These things are impossible in view of my propositions. God is just using them for His own purposes ("Thou hast ordained them for judgment; thou hast established them for correction"); and He is carrying out those purposes. I do not understand it fully, but I am quite sure we are not going to be exterminated. This will not be the end of the story of Israel, although, from the description, there are apparently going to be very few of us left, and we are going to be carried into captivity. But a remnant will remain, because the Almighty is still God, and He is using the Chaldeans to do something within the purpose of the covenant. God is not showing weakness. He is not being defeated. God, because He is what He is, is doing this and doing it for His own grand end and object.'

II. THE PROBLEM OF RECONCILING GOD'S USE OF THE CHALDEANS WITH HIS HOLY CHARACTER

But let us come to the second problem. If God is all-powerful, and if He is in control of events, how can these events be reconciled with His holy character? If we admit the power of God, and see that the Chaldeans are but instruments in His hands, and that their success is not due to their own god, we must still ask how a holy God can allow such things to take place? Habakkuk applies the same method as before.

(a) A holy God hates sin and can do no evil

He starts by saying, ' I am sure of this—" Thou art of purer eyes than to behold evil, and canst not look on iniquity " (i. 13). Whatever else I am uncertain of, I know that God cannot look upon evil without hating it. He detests it.' All evil in the world is utterly abhorrent to God because of His purity; He is of purer eyes than to behold evil with complacency. God and evil are eternal opposites. Anything unjust or cruel is far removed from the character of God. There is no question of there being injustice in God. He not only tempts no man, but He cannot be tempted with evil. ' God is light and in Him is no darkness at all.'

Having affirmed this, he turns immediately to the perplexing difficulty. ' If this is true of thee, O God,' he says, ' wherefore lookest thou upon them that deal treacherously and holdest thy tongue when the wicked devoureth the man that is more righteous than he?' How could God allow these Chaldeans to do this to His own people? The prophet's own people might be bad, but the Chaldeans were worse. Or, to put it in its modern form, Christians say: ' I am ready to admit the Church has been backsliding for years, but the Communists are godless. How can God allow the things which are happening?' Or to apply it more personally, men often protest: ' I admit I am not everything I might be; but so and so is worse, and yet he is prospering.' What is the reply?

c

(b) *Therefore I commit the unsolved problem to God*

In this particular paragraph in the prophecy, no
answer is given. To the first question about the power
of God the prophet received a positive answer. But
this problem of the holiness of God is more difficult.
After stating his absolutes and bringing his problem into
this context, there is still no clear answer. Now in
experience it is often like that. You apply the same
method which has worked so well in other cases, but
there is no immediate answer. What does one do in
such a case? Certainly do not rush to conclusions and
say, ' Because I do not understand it therefore I wonder
whether God is righteous after all.' No! If you still
do not understand, after applying the God-given
methods, then talk to God about it. We make a mistake when we talk to ourselves and then to other people,
and ask, ' Why this? Isn't it strange?' We must do
what the prophet did: take the problem to God and
leave it with Him.

(c) *The example of the Son of God*

A Christian may be kept in this position for a week,
or months, or years. It has often so happened. But
leave it with God! This is not only the prophetic
method; it was the attitude adopted by the Son of God
Himself when He was in this world. The problem for
Him was that of being ' made sin ' for man's salvation.
He knew that His Father could have delivered Him
out of the hands, not only of the Jews, but of the Romans
also. He could have commanded twelve legions of
angels and escaped. But if He was to be made sin, and
sin was to be punished in His body, it meant that He
must be separated from the Father. That was the
problem; and the Son of God was faced with the greatest
perplexity of His human life on earth. The one thing

from which He shrank was separation from the Father. But what did He do? Precisely what the prophet did; He prayed and said, 'O my Father, if it be possible, let this cup pass from me: nevertheless not as I will, but as thou wilt' (Mt. xxvi. 39). 'I do not understand it,' He said in effect, 'but if it is Thy way, very well, I am going on.' He took the problem He did not understand to God and left it there. We may say with reverence that the Lord Jesus, though perhaps not fully understanding because He had been made man, nevertheless went on, confident that God's will is always right, and that a holy God will never command anything that is wrong.

CHAPTER THREE

WAITING FOR GOD'S ANSWER

Habakkuk ii. 1–3

I. THE ATTITUDE OF FAITH

AFTER telling God about his perplexity in Habakkuk i the prophet goes on to say, in chapter ii, ' I will stand upon my watch, and set me upon the tower, and will watch to see what he will say unto me, and what I shall answer when I am reproved ' (ii. 1). The last phrase may mean, ' what I shall answer when I am reproved by those who will not like my message,' or ' when I am reproved by God for what I have said ', or ' what He will say unto me when He answers my complaint.' But the important consideration is that Habakkuk now realizes that the one thing to do is to wait upon God. It is not enough just to pray, to tell God about our perplexities, and just to cast our burden on the Lord. We must go further and wait upon God.

(a) Commit your problem to God

What does this mean in practice? First, *we must detach ourselves from the problem.* The prophet's words suggest that interpretation by picturing a tower set upon a high elevation which commands a wide view and a grand prospect, such as is used by military observers in order to anticipate the arrival of an enemy. The watchman is far above the plains and the crowds of people, occupying a point of vantage where he can see everything that is happening. ' I will watch to see what he will say unto me.' Now here is one of the most important principles in the psychology of the Christian life, or the understanding of how to fight in the spiritual conflict. Once we have taken a problem to God, we should cease to concern ourselves with it. We should turn our backs upon it and centre our gaze upon God.

Is not this precisely where we go astray? We have a perplexity, and we have applied the prophetic method of laying down postulates and putting the problem in the context of those propositions which we have laid down. But still we do not find satisfaction, and we do not quite know what to do. It may be the problem of what we are to do with our lives; or it may be some situation that is confronting us which involves a difficult decision. Having failed to reach a solution, despite seeking the guidance of the Holy Spirit, there is nothing more to do but to take it to God in prayer. But what so frequently happens is this. We go on our knees and tell God about the thing that is worrying us; we tell Him that we cannot solve the difficulty ourselves, that we cannot understand; and we ask Him to deal with it and to show us His way. Then the moment we get up from our knees we begin to worry about the problem again.

Now if you do that, you might just as well not have prayed. If you take your problem to God, leave it with God. You have no right to brood over it any longer. In his perplexity, Habakkuk says, ' I am going to get out of this vale of depression; I am going to the watch-tower; I am going up to the heights; I am going to look to God and to God alone '—one of the most important secrets of the Christian life! If you have committed your problem to God and go on thinking about it, it means that your prayers were not genuine.

If you told God on your knees that you had reached an impasse, and that you could not solve your problem, and that you were handing it over to Him, then leave it with Him. Resolutely refuse to think about it or talk about it. Do not go to the first Christian you meet and say, ' You know, I have an awful problem; I don't know what to do.' Don't discuss it. Leave it with God, and go on to the watch-tower. This may not be easy for us. We may have to be almost violent in forcing ourselves to do this. It is none the less essential. We must never allow ourselves to become submerged by a difficulty, to be shut in by the problem. We must come right out of it—' I will stand upon my watch, and set me upon the tower.' We have to extricate ourselves deliberately, to haul ourselves out of it, as it were, to detach ourselves from it altogether, and then take our stand looking to God—not at the problem.

There are endless illustrations of this important principle in the life of faith in the Scriptures themselves, and in Christian biography. Looking to God means not dealing with a problem yourself, not consulting other people, but depending entirely upon God, and ' waiting ' only upon Him.

Habakkuk looked at this problem but he could see no light. He was confronted by the fact that God was going to take up those appalling Chaldeans, people altogether worse than his own nation, and was going to use them for His own purpose. He could not understand it, nor reconcile it with the holiness of God. But he could and did take it to God. Having done so, he looked to God and ceased to look at his difficulty. That is the true basis of spiritual peace. That is exactly what Paul meant in Philippians, ' in nothing be anxious ' (see Phil. iv. 6, 7). It does not matter what the cause is; never let yourself be anxious, and never let yourself be burdened or worn down by care. You have no right to be perturbed; you must never have that anxious care that is not only spiritually crippling but also physically debilitating. Never be anxious but ' in every thing '—it is all-inclusive—' by prayer and supplication with thanksgiving let your requests be made known unto God.' And then, ' the peace of God, which passeth all understanding, shall keep your hearts and minds through Christ Jesus.' Get up into your watch-tower and just keep looking up to God. Look at nothing else, least of all your problem.

(b) Expect an answer from God

But we must go further and *we must look for the answer*. ' I will watch to see,' says this man. The military watchman's task is to keep his eye on that landscape in front for the slightest indication of movement on the part of the enemy. Habakkuk is looking for the answer. We so often fail because we just pray to God and then forget about it. If we pray to God we must expect answers to our prayers. Do we in fact, after we have prayed, continue to look to God and eagerly await the answer? Are we like this man on his watch-tower, expecting it to come at any moment?

God, of course, may answer in a number of different ways. For instance, you can expect God to answer you as you read His Word, for it is the commonest way of all in which He does this. As you are reading Scripture, suddenly a strange and wonderful light is cast upon your problem. If you say to yourself, ' This is the Word of God through which He speaks to men and I wonder what He has to say to me,' then you are likely to obtain your answer. Watch and wait for it.

Then God sometimes answers directly in our spirits. The prophet said: ' I will watch to see what He will say *in* me' (cf. AV margin). God speaks to me by speaking in me. He can so lay something upon the mind that we are certain of the answer. He can impress something upon our spirits in an unmistakable manner. We find ourselves unable to get away from an impression that is on our mind or heart; we try to rid ourselves of it, but back it comes. So does God answer at times.

Then again He sometimes answers our prayers by so providentially ordering our circumstances, and the day-to-day happenings of our lives, that it becomes quite plain what God is saying. God never calls us to do any work without opening the door. He may take a long time, but if God wants us to do some special task He will shut other doors and open that particular one. Our whole life will be directed to that end. This is a common experience of the Christian life. God often allows obstacles to arise, but the way ahead remains clear. God's will is certain. The point is that we must be *looking* for these answers, and ready to recognize them when they come. Having committed my problem to God I must expect God to answer. I should also compare one indication of guidance with another, because if God is always consistent with Himself in His dealings with me, I can expect them all to converge.

(c) *Watch and wait for the answer*

The third and last principle illustrated for us is that *we must watch eagerly and persistently*, like this watchman upon his tower. We must believe that God is always true to His word, and that His promises never fail. So, having committed myself and my problem to God, I must persist in looking with an eagerness which knows that God is certain to answer. It is dishonouring to God not to do so. If I believe God is my Father, and

that the very hairs of my head are all numbered, and
that God is much more concerned about my welfare
and my well-being than I am myself; if I believe that
God is much more concerned about the honour of His
great and holy name than I am, then it is surely dishonouring to God not to look for an answer after I
have prayed to Him. It is indicative of a serious lack of
faith. Nothing so shows the character of our faith as
our conduct and attitude after we have prayed. The
men of faith not only prayed, but they expected
answers. Sometimes, in a panic, we pray to God; then,
after the panic is over, we forget all about it. The test
of our faith is whether we expect an answer. The
prophet stood upon his watch, and set him upon the
tower. Though he could not understand God's actions,
he took the problem to God and then looked for an
answer.

II. FAITH REWARDED

Verses 2 and 3 of chapter ii contain the answer
Habakkuk was given. ' Write the vision, and make it
plain upon tables, that he may run that readeth it. For
the vision is yet for an appointed time, but at the end
it shall speak, and not lie: though it tarry, wait for it;
because it will surely come, it will not tarry.' This
lesson is invaluable. It is an absolute law in the
spiritual realm that if we adopt Habakkuk's method,
and behave as he behaved, God will always honour His
promises. In effect, God said, ' It is all right, Habakkuk,
I have heard your prayer, I understand your perplexity. Here is My answer. The Chaldeans whom I
am going to raise up to punish Israel will themselves in
turn be completely routed and destroyed.' The greatness of the Chaldeans was going to be short-lived. It
was God who for a special purpose raised them up; but

they took the glory to themselves and became inflated with a sense of their own power. Then God struck, and raised up the Medes and Persians who utterly destroyed the Chaldeans. God told the prophet to write the prophecy very clearly, so that any one reading it could at once understand and run to obey and warn others.

III. THE TRUE NATURE OF PROPHECY

We now come to the general subject of prophecy. In approaching our contemporary problem about the nature of history and the biblical philosophy of history, it is of the first importance to understand the true nature of prophecy. Prophecy occupies a large place in the Bible. There is certainly nothing that will bring greater comfort and consolation to the believer than to understand the nature of prophecy. Prophecy is basic in relation to the teaching of the Bible about God's revelation to man. That is why, during the last hundred years, the attack upon the true Christian faith has generally concentrated on this very subject. Unbelief is always critical of prophecy. The teaching of the Scriptures about the miracles of the Bible is alike pivotal to the whole position of the true evangelical faith. Consequently, rationalism has been very concerned to deny both the scriptural view of prophecy and the miracles of the Bible since these are the supreme manifestations of the supernatural element in history and in the Bible.

(a) *It is God's revelation to man*

Prophecy, then, is declared in the book of Habakkuk to be first of all *something that is revealed by God to man.* ' Write the vision, and make it plain.' God revealed

to Habakkuk what was going to take place. Rationa-
lists (some of whom call themselves Christian and
sometimes even occupy prominent positions in the
Church) dislike that idea entirely. Their explanation
of prophecy is that the Old Testament prophets were
simply men with political genius and a particularly clear
insight into the situation. They dispute the very idea
that God *revealed* things to these men at all. They claim
that the prophets were profound political thinkers,
great philosophers, or men with intuitive, almost in-
stinctive, insight into affairs. They admit, of course,
that the prophets were quite exceptional men, but
consider that they simply possessed, as a poet does,
particularly clear insight. They saw the inner meaning
of what was happening, and wrote what they saw.
That, however, is not the teaching of the Bible which
makes it clear that the very essence of prophecy is that
God took hold of a certain man and gave him a message. God said to Habakkuk, for instance: ' You have
brought your problem to me and I am going to give you
an answer.' It was a divine revelation.

In 2 Peter i. 20 it clearly states ' that no prophecy of
the scripture is of any private interpretation ', which
means that it is not something that man thinks out for
himself, or divines, or excogitates. It is not something
that proceeds from the mind of man. Prophecy was
the result of holy men speaking as they were moved,
or carried along by the Holy Ghost. Now Peter was
concerned to comfort Christians who were perplexed,
very much as Habakkuk was and as we are today, at
what was happening, and he urges them to pay particular attention to the word of prophecy—' we have also
a more sure word of prophecy ' (2 Peter i. 19). They
should understand what was meant by prophecy. It
was not something the Old Testament prophets thought

out, but something given them by the Holy Spirit to transmit to others. Prophecy is not private interpretation of events but God revealing truth to man.

(b) It is a foretelling of events

A second element contained in prophecy is that of *fore-telling*. The critics, again, object to that. They would define prophecy not as a fore-telling, but only as ' forth-telling ', or a form of teaching. Prophecy is, of course, a forth-telling, and a form of teaching, but an essential fact about this form of teaching is that the prophet fore-tells, or predicts, what is going to happen in the future. God told Habakkuk two things long before they came to pass: that He was going to raise up the Chaldeans and that, after they had conquered Israel and were enjoying international supremacy, they were going to be suddenly destroyed. We must insist that such cardinal events were revealed in advance to the prophets whom God raised up from time to time to warn and to reprove Israel.

(c) It is certain of fulfilment

There is another element, which is of supreme consolation to the believer: the fulfilment of prophecy is *certain*. ' Write the vision, and make it plain upon tables . . . for the vision is yet for an appointed time.' The events foretold are certain to take place in due course, and in God's time. ' Though it tarry, wait for it.' It may tarry and there may be delay, but nothing can prevent or frustrate the fulfilment . ' It will surely come ' said God. The people must be told. What God has promised, He will most certainly perform. There is a tone of complete finality in all Bible prophecy.

(d) It is of exact fulfilment

The last element in prophecy, perhaps the most wonderful of all, is that it is *exact*—' Write the vision . . . make it plain . . . for the vision is yet for an appointed time, but at the end it shall speak, and not lie '. The time for the fulfilment is fixed. The exact moment is determined by God. It will not be late. This is a very vital principle in connection with prophecy. God not only fore-tells what is going to happen, and reveals it to His servant, and reminds him that it is absolutely certain, but He adds that it will take place at the exact minute appointed, and that it will not be a fraction of a second late.

If we want to keep calm and even joyful in these difficult times in which we are living, it is vital that we should grasp the great principles of divine prophecy. The Old Testament is full of it. Notice how God foretold the flood. A hundred and twenty years passed and nothing seemed to be more unlikely. The people laughed at Noah for expecting it. But at the appointed time it came. So it was in the case of Sodom and Gomorrah. There was a divinely pre-determined moment, and when the time came, God acted. The most striking example is found in the life of Abraham. In the fifteenth chapter of the book of Genesis we find this statement: ' Know of a surety that thy seed shall be a stranger in a land that is not theirs, and shall serve them; and they shall afflict them four hundred years; And also that nation, whom they shall serve, will I judge: and afterward shall they come out with great substance ' (verses 13, 14). Later, in Ex. xii. 40, 41, we read: ' Now the sojourning of the children of Israel, who dwelt in Egypt, was four hundred and thirty years. And it came to pass at the end of the four hundred and thirty years, even the selfsame day it came to pass, that all the hosts of the Lord went out from the land of Egypt.' How exact!—' the selfsame day '. So also in Habakkuk's case, there will not be a second's delay. God has fixed ' the appointed time '. Then to Jeremiah it was revealed that his nation was going to be kept in Babylon for exactly seventy years, at the end of which the people would be brought back. It all came to pass. Similarly, Daniel was enabled of God to prophesy with exactness the time of the coming of the Son of God, the Messiah.

So wait upon God. He will certainly send the answer. Everything He has ordained will certainly and most surely come to pass, and at the exact time appointed for it.

For Christian people today, in perplexity with regard to so much that is happening in the Church and in the world, this is still the answer of God. Not only is the whole future course of history known to God, and His purpose for the Church made plain, but what He has decreed will most certainly come to pass. It may at times be difficult to understand the delay. Yet, ' with God a thousand years are as one day and one day as a thousand years.' Wait for the vision; it is certain, it is sure, it can never fail.

CHAPTER FOUR

'THE JUST SHALL LIVE BY FAITH'

Habakkuk ii. 4–20 (especially verses 4, 14 and 20)

THE import of the message from verse 4 to the end of chapter ii is that the Chaldeans, who were going to be used as an instrument to chastise Israel, were themselves going to be chastised and finally routed. God was using them temporarily, but their final end was certain. God was going to humble the pride of the Chaldeans and inflict a terrible punishment upon them. The details given in these verses describe the arrogance and the foulness of the Chaldeans with an exactness which is confirmed from secular history. To understand the teaching we must emphasize certain principles clearly taught here.

I. HISTORICAL EVENTS MUST BE INTERPRETED IN THE LIGHT OF GOD'S KINGDOM

The important thing for us is to see the relevance of all this for ourselves. The case in question is an illustration of a universal principle in God's dealings with mankind. In the present world situation a proper understanding of this principle is especially urgent. If we desire to be at peace within, in spite of what is happening in the world round and about us, the only way to do so is to understand this biblical philosophy of history which explains what is happening in the secular world and its bearing on the Church of God. The essential principle is that history can be understood only in terms of God's kingdom—that is, the rule of God in the world as a whole and including the Church. All history is being directed by God in order to bring His own purpose with respect to the kingdom to pass. Our object now is to look at this principle in greater detail.

II. PERPLEXITY AT CURRENT EVENTS NO NEW EXPERIENCE

The problem is not a new one. We, in this twentieth century, have been foolish enough to imagine that our problems are exceptional and peculiar. They are not. We are experiencing only what God's people have experienced many a time before. It is well to remember that history repeats itself, and so get rid of that foolish, inflated opinion that we moderns have of ourselves. Our perplexities are by no means new. There are many people today who feel that they cannot be Christians because of the intellectual difficulties raised by the apparent frustration of history. But this problem is as old as man himself, and has perplexed people right from the beginning. Modern knowledge and modern events have really little to do with it, so let us first get rid of any pride of intellect. The problem is the same as that of the man who wrote the seventy-third Psalm,[1] or Habakkuk, or Israel in general. The Epistle to the Hebrews was written specifically to elucidate this problem. 'Here we are,' said the Hebrew Christians, in effect; 'we believed your gospel, we left Judaism and joined the Christian Church because of what you told us about Christ and His salvation, and about His coming to establish His kingdom and to reign on the earth. But He has not come: we are being persecuted, and despoiled of our goods, and having a very hard time. What is the answer?'

[1] Ps. lxxiii. 11, 12, 13ff.

The Christians to whom Peter wrote were tempted to echo, ' Where is the promise of His coming ? ' because they were being taunted by the scoffers who said: ' Ah, you believed this gospel and trusted yourself to this Lord Jesus Christ. You have been told that He is coming back to reign; but where is the promise of His coming? Everything seems to be going on as it was! ' And it is noteworthy that Peter reminds his leaders that it was an old problem. He said: ' It is all right, don't listen to them. It is exactly what people said before the Flood; it is what they said before the destruction of Sodom and Gomorrah; it is what they have always said.' His answer was: ' One day is with the Lord as a thousand years, and a thousand years as one day. The Lord is not slack concerning His promise, as some men count slackness.' Now that is precisely what Habakkuk says: ' The vision is yet for an appointed time, but at the end it shall speak, and not lie: though it tarry, wait for it; because it will surely come, it will not tarry.'

The historical theme is also the one great theme of the book of the Revelation. However you interpret the book, it is clearly a forecast of history, a pre-view of relevant events through the long course of history until the final consummation. But many interpreters become so obsessed with the symbolism that they miss the main theme. They are so expert in the details that they lose the central truth. They fail to see the wood for the trees. The book of Revelation is primarily a great preview of history, with the Lord Jesus Christ as the One who controls history opening ' the Seals '. It thus contains a message of consolation, not only for first-century Christians, but for Christ's people at all times and in all places.

D

III. TWO POSSIBLE WAYS OF LIFE: THE WAY OF REASON
AND THE WAY OF FAITH

Turning to the passage under consideration, verse 4 reads: ' but the just shall live by his faith.' You will remember that this important statement is quoted several times in the New Testament. Scholars disagree as to the exact translation of the first part of the verse. Either it can be ' His soul which is lifted up is not upright in him ' (AV) or, as quoted in Heb. x. 38, where it is stated that God has no pleasure in the soul of him that draws back (or withdraws himself). The truth stated is that there are only two possible attitudes to life in this world: that of faith and that of unbelief. Either we view our lives in terms of our belief in God, and the conclusions which we are entitled to draw from that; or our outlook is based upon a rejection of God and the corresponding denials. We may either ' withdraw ' ourselves from the way of faith in God, or else we may live by faith in God. The very terms suggest corresponding ways of life. As a man believes so is he. A man's belief determines his conduct. The just, the righteous, shall live by faith; or, in other words, the man who lives by faith is righteous. On the other hand, the man who ' draws back ' is unrighteous because he is not living by faith. Here is the great watershed of life, and all of us are on one side of it or the other. Whatever my political or philosophical views may be, they must have this common denominator: either my life is based on faith or it is not. If it is not, it does not much matter what my views may be, or whether I am controlled by political, social, economic, or any other considerations. What matters is whether I am accepting God's rule or not. The famous tenth, eleventh and twelfth chapters of the Epistle to the Hebrews expound and illustrate this truth.

There are two possibilities before each of us as we look out upon the world today and ponder the future course of history. I can observe and meditate upon what I see and then, after reading what military and political experts, statesmen and others write, I can finally turn to my history books. As a result I can make an attempt to draw my own conclusions and form my own opinions. Surely that is why most of us read newspaper articles! We say, ' This man is an expert; what does he think about it? ' There were experts who said there would not be a war in 1939. They claimed to have worked it out, and their considered opinion was that Hitler was unlikely to go to war. Many people accepted this opinion and made their business or other plans accordingly. They were governed by their own observations, and deductions, the application of common sense and a kind of worldly wisdom, or by the political acumen of certain prognosticators.

There is, however, another way of looking at things clearly taught in the Bible. It is not based upon conclusions drawn from the number of military divisions a country has or has not, or whether the time has yet come for some country to strike or not. The Bible simply states that a certain thing will happen! It gives no reason. It just says that it will happen because God says so. That is the case before us as it concerned the Chaldeans. No arguments are given; no careful balancing of the strength of the rival forces; nothing but the bare statement of God to the prophet. And the prophet believes it and acts upon it.

IV. THE UNAVOIDABLE NECESSITY OF CHOOSING BETWEEN THESE ALTERNATIVES

The lives of all of us are based on one or other of these two attitudes. Either I take the bare Word of God and live by it, or else I do not. If you protest against the idea that prophets can foretell the future, or that miracles and belief in the supernatural are unthinkable in a scientific, sophisticated age like this, you are just withdrawing from the godly way of life. The biblical way is living by faith. 'The just shall live by his faith.' Faith means taking the bare Word of God and acting upon it because it is the Word of God. It means believing what God says simply and solely because He has said it. Those heroes of the faith in Heb. xi believed the Word of God simply because God had spoken. They had no other reason for believing it. Why, for example, did Abraham take Isaac and go with him up that mountain? Why was he on the point of sacrificing his son? Simply because God had told him to do so.

But living by faith means even more than that. It means basing the whole of our life upon faith in God. The secret of all those Old Testament characters was that they lived ' as seeing him who is invisible '. They preferred, like Moses, to ' suffer affliction with the people of God than to enjoy the pleasures of sin for a season '. On the one hand, in the court of Egypt, there was worldly wisdom; and on the other, the bare Word of God which had revealed to Moses His purposes for the people to whom he belonged, and the destiny for which He was preparing them. At the time they were slaves and being cruelly treated. Moses had only the bare Word of God to act upon; but he forsook the court of Pharaoh and, turning his back upon wonderful prospects, went out, like Abraham, forsaking his own country. He went out ' as seeing him who is invisible '. ' The just shall live by faith.' These men staked all on God's Word. They were prepared to suffer for it, and if necessary endure the loss of all things. The same prospect faced many of the early

Christians. They were placed in a terrible predicament. They were asked to say ' Caesar is Lord '. But they said, ' We cannot say it because we know that he is not; there is only one Lord, the Lord Jesus Christ! ' ' If you do not say Caesar is Lord,' said the authorities, ' you will be thrown to the lions in the arena! ' Still they refused to say it. On what grounds? On the grounds of the bare Word of God! They believed that a certain Person had been born into this world in great poverty in Bethlehem, had worked as a carpenter and eventually died upon a cross. But, they also believed that He was the Lord of glory and that He had risen from the dead. And on the strength of that they declared that they would never say that Caesar was Lord. They risked all. They died by faith and in faith.

This is our position as Christians today. The choice is being forced upon us more and more. Is there anyone still foolish enough to bank on this world and what it has to offer? What is the controlling principle in our lives? Is it calculation? Is it worldly wisdom— a shrewd, balanced view based on history and human knowledge? Or is it the Word of God, warning us that this life and this world are only transient, and that both are merely a preparation for the world to come? It does not tell us to turn our backs entirely upon the world, but it does insist that we have the right view of the world. It emphatically states that what really matters is the coming of God's kingdom. We must ask ourselves, as in the presence of God, the simple questions: Is my life based upon the faith principle? Am I submitting myself to the fact that what I read in the Bible is the Word of God and is true? And am I willing to stake everything, my life included, upon this fact? For ' the just shall live by faith '.

V. THE ABSOLUTE CERTAINTY OF THE DESTRUCTION OF EVIL AND THE TRIUMPH OF GOD

The five woes recorded in this chapter are true not only with respect to the Chaldeans, but as a universal principle in history. Everything that is evil is under the judgment of God. Though the Chaldeans were to be raised up to flourish for a while, the limit of their prosperity was absolutely fixed. The wicked may triumph for a while, they may 'flourish as the green bay tree', but it is not going to last. Their doom is sealed. What perplexes God's people is, Why does God allow it? He allows it for His own purposes, so that the world may stagger under these evil powers, before He suddenly shows His power and manifests His own sovereignty. The principle for us to hold on to is that God is over all. 'The way of the transgressor is hard' whether it be an individual, a nation, or the whole world. Your worldly man may make a fortune by evil business methods and arrive at the top. But see the end of the ungodly! Look at him dying upon his bed; see him buried in a grave, and think of the doom and woe that are his destiny! We should feel sorry for the ungodly that they are fools enough to become drunk with temporal success. Their end is fixed.

And so with nations. Read in your secular history books about the godless imperial nations that have risen, and how they seemed to have the whole world at their feet—Egypt, Babylon, Greece, Rome! But recall their end. During the Christian era the same thing has happened. There was a time when the Turks looked as if they were going to master the whole world; but eventually they fell. Nation after nation has risen only to fall. The time came when the woe pronounced by

God was put into effect. We ourselves have lived
through an era in which we have seen this very principle
in operation. And whatever may be happening in the
world today, the principle is still operative. Woe is
declared upon the ways of all opposed to God. They
are doomed. They may have great temporary success,
and we must be prepared for that; they may apparently
bestride the universe, but as certainly as their star arose
it will go down. The woe, the judgment, the doom of
God upon the unrighteous is certain.

Turning to the positive aspect of this truth (verse 14)
we read, ' For the earth shall be filled with the knowledge of the glory of the Lord, as the waters cover the
sea '. It is not for anyone to attempt to predict what
is going to happen in detail, but we can be certain of
one great fact, namely the *ultimate triumph of God*.

> ' Jesus shall reign where'er the sun
> Doth his successive journeys run.
> His kingdom stretch from shore to shore
> Till moons shall wax and wane no more.'

Yes, the heathen may rage, and the people imagine a
vain thing, ' Yet have I set my king upon my holy hill
of Zion.' Let the enemies of God and His people be
rampant; let everything appear as if they are going to
exterminate the Christian Church! Yet a day is certainly coming when ' at the name of Jesus every knee
shall bow, of things in heaven, and things in earth, and
things under the earth; and every tongue shall confess
that Jesus Christ is Lord to the glory of God the Father '.
Certainly the earth shall be filled with the glory of God.
The Evil One will be routed and cast into the lake of
fire; everything opposed to God will be destroyed, and
there will be ' a new heaven and a new earth, wherein
dwelleth righteousness '. The city of God will descend,

and the just shall enter in. Everything unclean will be shut outside, and God will be all and in all. The ultimate triumph of God is sure.

In the light of all this, what, then, is our final conclusion? 'What profiteth the graven image that the maker thereof hath graven it; the molten image, and a teacher of lies, that the maker of his work trusteth therein, to make dumb idols?' (verse 18). God forbid that we should trust, or commit ourselves to, any power other than God Himself, to any idols man may set up, even though they be the British Commonwealth of Nations or the United Nations! 'Woe unto him that saith to the wood, Awake; to the dumb stone, Arise, it shall teach! Behold, it is laid over with gold and silver, and there is no breath at all in the midst of it' (verse 19). .Put your trust in nothing of man, but in God alone!

'But the Lord is in his holy temple: let all the earth keep silence before him' (verse 20). Not only must the heathen be silent, but Christians must keep silent too. There must be no querying, no questioning, no uncertainty about the goodness and the holiness and the power of God. Do not complainingly ask, 'Why does God allow this?' or 'Why does God do that?' Consider the Word of the Lord to His prophet. Look up to God. Look at the ultimate and the absolute. Then let us put our hands upon our mouths that are so ready to speak foolishly. Let us realize that He is there in the temple of the universe, God over all. Let us silently humble ourselves and bow down before Him and worship Him. Let us magnify His grace, His might, His power, His goodness, and in quiet peace of heart and mind and soul wait for Him.

CHAPTER FIVE

HOW TO PRAY

Habakkuk iii. 1, 2

I. THE CHARACTER OF TRUE PRAYER

THE response to God's foregoing revelation to Habakkuk is described as a prayer. But it is at the same time a wonderful piece of poetry, entitled ' A prayer of Habakkuk the prophet upon Shigionoth '. It was a prayer accompanied with music, neither mournful, nor joyful, but expressive of profound and strong emotion. The prophet was undoubtedly moved to the very depths of his being with conflicting emotions, predominantly those of triumph and victory.

The whole of the chapter is a record of the prophet's prayer. Prayer is more than petition, and includes praise, thanksgiving, recollection and adoration. The very invoking of history, as we find the prophet doing here, is often an essential part of prayer. The great prayers of the Bible are those of men who reminded God of what He had done in the past. They based their petitions upon those facts. This entire chapter, then, is a great prayer.

But the second verse of this chapter is a model of what the Christian's attitude should always be at a time of trouble or crisis. Today we are confronted by a world situation which may well prompt the spiritually minded to think of this book of Habakkuk. Our problem is again: Why doesn't God intervene? Why does God allow these things? Why are the ungodly so

successful? Why doesn't God come to revive the
Church? In face of these things our attitude shouid
be that of the prophet. Is it so? Was it so even in
the dark days of the last war? Was our response to the
so-called days of national prayer the response which
we find here, or in the ninth chapter of the book of
Daniel? There was, we must admit, a most vital
element lacking in the attitude of the Christian Church
and in the nation at those times. Certain subtle
dangers always confront the Christian, as they confronted the prophet Habakkuk. The devil, as ' an
angel of light ', seeks to take advantage of every perplexity, making us look at the wrong things and so
warping our attitude towards God. The attitude
which should characterize Christian people in a time
of trial and perplexity is seen here.

II. THE ESSENTIAL ELEMENTS IN TRUE PRAYER

(a) *Humiliation*

We first notice *the self-humbling of the prophet*, or *his
attitude of humility*. ' O Lord,' he says, ' I have heard
thy speech, and was afraid: O Lord, revive thy work
in the midst of the years, in the midst of the years make
known; in wrath remember mercy.' There is no
longer any arguing with God or questioning His ways
as at first. He does not even protest at what God has
told him. From intellectual perplexity he has pro-
gressed to a position above and beyond it. He does
not even appeal to God to reverse the purpose of judgment. There is no request whatsoever that God should
hold His hand, or spare Israel. We find, rather, a
recognition that what God says He will do is perfectly
right; that God is absolutely just, and that the punishment which is going to come upon Israel is well

deserved—an attitude of complete submission to the
will of God.[1] There is no attempt to defend Israel or
himself, but frank admission of sin and a recognition
of the righteousness, holiness and justice of God. ' To
us,' he says, ' belongs confusion of face.' Not a vestige
of self-righteousness remains, just complete admission
of sin and utter submission to the judgment of God
upon the nation.

How was Habakkuk brought to such a position? It
would seem that it was when he stopped thinking of his
own nation, or of the Chaldeans, and contemplated
only the holiness and justice of God against the dark
background of sin in the world. Our troubles can
nearly all be traced to our persistence in looking at the
immediate problems themselves, instead of looking at
them in the light of God. So long as Habakkuk was
looking at Israel and the Chaldeans, he was troubled.
Now he has forgotten Israel as such, and the Chaldeans,
and his eyes are on God. He has returned to the realm
of spiritual truth—the holiness of God, sin in man and
in the world—and so he is able to see things in an
entirely new light. He is now concerned for the glory
of God and for nothing else. He had to stop thinking
in terms of fact that the Chaldeans were worse sinners
than the Jews and that yet God was going to use them,
perplexing though this problem was. That attitude
made him forget the sin of his own nation through concentrating on the sin of others which happened to be
greater. As long as he persisted in this attitude he
remained in perplexity, unhappy in heart and mind.
But the prophet came to the place where he was lifted
entirely out of that state, to see only the wonderful
vision of the Lord in His holy temple, with sinful mankind and the universe beneath Him. The distinction

[1] Cf. Daniel's prayer in Dn. ix.

between the Israelites and the Chaldeans became rela-
tively unimportant when things were seen like that.
It was no longer possible to be exalted either as an
individual or as a nation. When things are seen from
a spiritual viewpoint, there can only be an acknow-
ledgment that ' All have sinned and come short of the
glory of God', and 'The whole world lieth in the evil
one '. The holiness of God and the sin of man are the
only things that matter.

Herein lies the crux of the situation at the present
time. Do we yet see our need of humiliation? Do we
see it as members of the Christian Church? Do we see
it as citizens of the nation? We are confronted by a
world situation in which we do not know what is going
to happen. Is there to be another war? If our attitude
is still one of ' Why does God allow this ? ', ' What have
we done to deserve this? ', we have manifestly not
learned the lesson Habakkuk learned. We did not truly
humble ourselves in the last war or in the first world war.
We failed to recognize that the two wars were the
inevitable consequence of the godlessness that had been
rampant for nearly a hundred years, all because of the
pride and arrogance of man. Has the Christian Church
realized that her present condition, and much of her
suffering, may be the chastisement of the Lord for the
infidelity and apostasy into which the Church herself
has frequently fallen? For a century the Church,
speaking generally, has been denying the supernatural
and the miraculous, questioning the very deity of
Christ and exalting philosophy over revelation. Is the
Church therefore in a position to complain if she is
having a hard time now? Has she humbled herself in
sackcloth and ashes? Has she acknowledged and con-
fessed her sin? Then has our nation, the nation that
has been so blessed of God, and so used of God, a right

to complain? How has she requited the God who has so blessed her? Realizing the godlessness and the departure from spiritual standards that is so true of our country, have we any right to protest? Has the world as a whole any right to complain? In spite of the judgments of God upon us, has there been a humbling? Is there a spirit of repentance? If so, where is it?

It is thoroughly unbiblical and unspiritual to look only at the obviously godless. Christian people, and even leaders, tend to give the impression that there is only one problem—that of Communism. They have fallen into the error into which Habakkuk fell for a while. One hears it said so frequently that ' the Christian Church isn't perfect, but look at Communism; the Church isn't all she ought to be, but look at *that*!' They therefore see no need for self-humiliation. Many see only one problem, that of the Chaldeans—the Communists—and so long as they are looking at them they are not ready to humble themselves. The lesson learned by the prophet Habakkuk was that it is no longer a question of nationalism or of antagonism to another nation. Nothing else matters except the holiness of God and sin. There is nothing to do but to humble ourselves in the sight of God. Nothing could be more disastrous, or more unbiblical, than for the Christian Church to conceive it as her main duty to oppose Communism, much less to be led into such a campaign by the Church of Rome. There is no such thing as unity between the Church and the State. These problems must be considered not politically, but spiritually. Our one concern must be with the holiness of God and the sin in man—whether found in the Church, in the State, or in the world. Whatever may be true of Communists, or of anybody else who is opposed to Christ, my first question must be: What about myself? Does the fact that there are others worse than I am mean that I am all right? Not as Daniel or Habakkuk saw it! All of us, like Habakkuk, must confess to God: 'We have sinned against Thee, and we have no right to plead any mitigation of the sentence in Thy holy presence.' Such a self-humbling in the presence of God is desperately needed.

(b) Adoration

But there is a second element in the prayer, that of *adoration*. 'O Lord, I have heard thy speech, and was afraid.' 'Was afraid' does not mean that Habakkuk was afraid of the things that were going to happen as revealed to him by God. There was no fear of the suffering that was coming. The expression suggests awe in the presence of such a great God, worshipful adoration and wonder at God and His ways. God had told him something about His historical plan, and the prophet, meditating upon the fact that God is in His holy temple and the world beneath His feet, stood in amazement and reverential awe. When he realized the almightiness and the holiness of God he said, ' I was afraid '. What is described in the Epistle to the Hebrews as an attitude of ' reverence and godly fear ' is an attitude strangely lacking amongst us, even among evangelicals. There is far too much easy familiarity with the Most High. Thank God, we can come into His presence with holy boldness through the blood of Christ. But that should never lessen our reverence and godly fear. God's ancient people, especially the most spiritual among them, were so conscious of the holiness and the greatness of God that they trembled even to use His name. The sanctity and the holiness and the almightiness of God was something which made them almost speechless—' I was afraid '. We should approach Him ' with reverence and godly fear, for our God is a consuming fire '.

This is essential for an understanding of the times in which we live. We must learn to see God in His holy temple above the flux of history, and above the changing scenes of time. In God's presence the one thing that stands out is the holy nature of God and our own sin. We humble ourselves and with reverence adore Him.

(c) Petition

Lastly, we come to *the element of petition*. ' In nothing be anxious,' says the apostle Paul, ' but in every thing by prayer and supplication with thanksgiving let your requests be made known unto God '. True prayer always includes these same three elements: humiliation, adoration, petition. What is the petition in Habakkuk's case? Not a petition for deliverance and ease, nor a petition that God will spare, nor that there may be no war against the Chaldeans; not that there may be no suffering, no sacking of Jerusalem, and no razing the temple to the ground. There was no such petition because he had come to see that these events were both inevitable, and well-deserved. He does not pray that God would change His plan. The prophet's one burden now was a concern for God's cause, God's work, and God's purpose in his own nation and in the entire world. His one desire was that things should be right. He had come to the position in which, in effect, he said, ' Whatever I and my countrymen may have to suffer is of no concern so long as *Thy work* is revived and kept pure.' His one great plea was that God would revive His work in the midst of the years—' O Lord, revive thy work in the midst of the years, in the midst of the years make known.'

The expression, 'in the midst of the years' must surely mean, 'while these terrible things prophesied are actually taking place amongst us' or 'in the midst of the years of suffering and calamity which Thou hast foretold, even then, O Lord, revive Thy work'. This is a most appropriate prayer for the Church of today. If we are not more concerned for the purity of the Church than with the fact that we are faced by the possibility of another war, that is a serious reflection upon our Christianity. What is it that is chiefly worrying us as Christians? Is it events in the world around us? Or is it the name and the glory of our Almighty God, the health and the condition of His Church, the prosperity and the future of His cause among men? For Habakkuk there was only one concern. In spite of what he knew was going to happen, he prayed for a reviving of God's cause in Israel.

The Hebrew word 'revive' has the primary meaning of 'preserve', or 'keep alive'. Habakkuk's great fear was that the Church was going to be destroyed altogether, so he prayed 'Preserve it, O God, keep it alive, don't let it be overwhelmed'. But to revive means not only to keep alive or to preserve, but also to purify and correct, to get rid of the evil. This is always an essential accompaniment whenever God revives. In the history of every revival, we read of God purifying, getting rid of the sin, the dross, and the things that were hindering His cause.

There is a further idea also that, while the Church is being preserved, purified and corrected, she is at the same time being prepared for deliverance. The prophet looks at the approaching calamity and says: 'O Lord, even while we are being chastised, prepare us for the deliverance that is to come. Make all Thy people worthy of Thy blessings.' 'Remember Thy work,' he seems to say, ' and make it as it is meant to be; let the Church function as it ought to function '. This prayer, like Daniel's also, was very literally answered even when they were in captivity in Babylon and in the hands of the Chaldeans. God answered the prayer for reviving through chastisement, and even during the time that chastisement was being administered.

Habakkuk's final appeal is most touching—' In wrath,' he says, ' remember mercy.' Matthew Henry points out that he does not turn to God and say, ' O Lord, I do see that this punishment was necessary, but I would remind Thee that we have tried to be good and that there have been worse times in our history.' He does not ask God to remember them because of any of their merits, but he asks Him in wrath to remember mercy. By ' wrath ' is meant God's perfect righteousness and justice. The only thing he does is to remind God of His own nature, and of that other aspect of His holy being—His mercy. He seems to say: ' Temper wrath with mercy. We have nothing to say but to ask that Thou shouldest act like Thyself, and in the midst of wrath shouldest have pity upon us.'

Here we have the model prayer for just such a time as this. In all our ' national days of prayer ' during the last war there seemed to be an assumption that *we* were all right, and all we had to do was to ask God to defeat our enemies who alone were all wrong. No place seemed to be given for any real humiliation, or confession of sin, or bemoaning of our utter sinfulness and departure from God. The message of this book is that until we truly humble ourselves, forgetting other people, and those who are worse than we are, until we see ourselves as we are in the sight of God, and confess our sins and commit ourselves into His Almighty hands, we have no right to look for peace and happiness. Until

E

the world learns these mighty lessons from the Word of God there is no hope for it. There will be wars and further wars. God grant us grace to accept this message from the Bible, and to learn to see things not politically but spiritually.

There is a personal application of this principle. We must face our personal situation in the same way by asking: Is there something in my life that is meriting the chastisement of God? Have I been what I ought to be? Let us examine ourselves and humble ourselves under the mighty hand of God, and be concerned chiefly about the state of our souls. The trouble is that we always look at the situation and the problem instead of trying to discover whether there is anything in our souls that leads God so to deal with us. The moment I become really concerned about the state of my soul, instead of my affliction, I am on the high road to God's blessing. The Epistle to the Hebrews declares that chastisement is a proof that we are God's children. 'Whom the Lord loveth, he chasteneth.' If we do not know what chastisement means we ought to be alarmed because, if we are children of God, He is concerned about us and is bringing us to perfection. If we do not listen to His appeals He will bring us by another way to His desired end. 'Whom the Lord loveth he chasteneth and scourgeth every son whom he receiveth.' When things are apparently going against us, the thing to do is not to look at the situation and ask questions, but to look at ourselves and say: 'What of my soul ? What is God saying to me and doing to me? What is it in me that is meriting all this?' After examining ourselves, and humbling ourselves, we should place ourselves in the hands of God and say 'Thy way, not mine, O Lord, however hard it be. My one concern is that my soul should be right. I ask only that in wrath Thou shouldest remember mercy. But, above all, go on with Thy work that my soul may be revived, and that I may become well-pleasing in Thy sight'.

That was the attitude of Habakkuk. That has been the attitude of all God's true prophets. That is always the attitude of the Church at every time of true reviving and spiritual awakening. And that is the only right, biblical and spiritual attitude for the Church and individual Christians at this present hour. We should think less about the menace of Communism or anything else that threatens the Church, and be more concerned about the health and purity of the Church: most of all about the holiness of God and the sin of man.

CHAPTER SIX

HOW TO REJOICE IN TRIBULATIONS

Habakkuk iii. 3–19

I. FAITH AND FEAR

'WHEN I heard, my belly trembled; my lips quivered at the voice: rottenness entered into my bones, and I trembled in myself, that I might rest in the day of trouble: when he cometh up unto the people, he will invade them with his troops' (verse 16). The prophet no longer has any theological or philosophical problems. He sees everything perfectly clearly; but he is only human after all, and seeing the judgments that are coming, he is filled with fear. How can he find inward peace when all these things are impending? How will he stand up to them? It is great comfort to know that these mighty prophets of God were but men like ourselves and subject to the same frailties as ourselves. We are inclined to think of them as men apart because of the greatness of their understanding. But if we do so we shall derive much less benefit from a consideration of their writings. Here, then, we get a glimpse into this man's character. He is honest enough to tell us that when he heard what God had to tell him he trembled like a leaf. Our Lord recognized this same human frailty when He said, 'the spirit indeed is willing but the flesh is weak.' We should thank God for this distinction between lack of faith and the weakness of the flesh. God's greatest men of faith often

quailed physically at certain prospects which confronted them. To see the truth and understand the
doctrines is most important, but despite this clear understanding we may still tremble physically. To do so
under certain terrible conditions does not necessarily
mean that you have no faith, though the devil will try
to persuade you so. If ever you are so tempted, remember Habakkuk! Habakkuk understood perfectly,
yet he trembled like a leaf through the sheer weakness
of his flesh.

II. GOD'S PROVISION FOR THE FEARFUL PROPHET

(a) *The example of God's servants*

God ' knoweth our frame; he remembereth that we
are dust '. He understands our human weakness, and
has made wonderful provision for us. First of all, He
graciously tells us that even His greatest servants have
known something of physical fear combined with faith
in His Word. We have seen that this was so with
Habakkuk. But even Abraham, the man of great
faith, knew at times what it was to be weak in the flesh.
David, too, admitted that the flesh seemed to be failing
him in spite of his faith. Jeremiah, like Habakkuk, was
given a dark prophecy to deliver, and felt at times that
he could not face the ordeal. The message was so
terrible that, though in spirit he was ready to give it,
his flesh naturally shrank from it. We get a glimpse of
John the Baptist languishing in the prison, tired,
suffering physically, and with these conditions reacting
upon his spirit. We observe it even in the case of the
mighty St. Paul. He tells us in the second Epistle to
the Corinthians that his flesh had no rest. He was
' troubled on every side; without were fightings, within
were fears'. And when he preached for the first time
in Corinth he did so ' in weakness, fear and much

trembling '. Such examples assure us that God understands us, and in His mercy will show us a way out of our difficulties.

(b) The gift of joy, not self-control

Now what can a man do in such a state of human weakness? What was there to sustain a man like this when the Chaldeans arrived and began to destroy the city? What was it that sustained the faithful remnant of the people of God when everything apparently was lost? It was not merely resignation or saying: ' Well, there is no use crying over spilt milk, or getting alarmed and excited, because we cannot do anything about it.' Nor was it just applying the principle of psychological detachment. It was not taking oneself in hand and saying: ' The best thing is not to think about it! Go to the pictures, read novels and don't think! '—a sort of escapism. Neither was it an attempt at being courageous. There is here no exhortation to courage. There is something infinitely greater than just making a mighty effort of the will and saying: ' I am not going to whimper or cry, I am going to be a man.' Habakkuk admits that his ' belly trembled ', his lips quivered at the voice, and rottenness entered into his bones.

Now ' psychological ' treatment differs greatly from the scriptural method. It is often sheer cruelty to a man who is in a state of uncontrolled fear to say to him, ' Pull yourself together'. If he could, he would, and the trembling would stop. But the prophet is in a state in which he is unable to control his physical reactions. He cannot stop himself trembling, try as he will. The methods which the world offers at such a time are effective only for certain people, and at a stage when their help is hardly necessary. They are of no value when a person is in this stage of utter physical alarm.

Instead of mere resignation, or plucking up one's courage, the Scripture shows that it is possible even under such conditions to be in a state of actual rejoicing: ' Although the fig tree shall not blossom, neither shall fruit be in the vines; the labour of the olive shall fail, and the fields shall yield no meat; the flock shall be cut off from the fold, and there shall be no herd in the stalls: yet I will rejoice in the Lord, I will joy in the God of my salvation ' (verses 17, 18). The Christian claims nothing less than that. Your man of the world may, if he is in a physically good condition, school himself to a state of resignation. He may put on a courageous air as many did during the last war, and as many will continue to do. And that as far as it goes is a commendable spirit. But, in contrast to that, the Christian is assured that though he may be a person who is physically disposed to be thoroughly alarmed, he may experience not only strength but positive joy in the midst of danger. He may ' rejoice in tribulation ' and be triumphant in the midst of the worst circumstances. That is the challenge of the Christian position. Herein we as Christians are to differ from the world. When hell is let loose, and the worst comes to the worst, we are to do more than ' put up with it ' or ' be steady '. We are to know a holy joy and manifest a spirit of rejoicing. We are to be ' more than conquerors ', instead of merely exercising self-control with the aid of an iron will. We are to rejoice in the Lord and to joy in the God of our salvation. Such a time is a test for our Christian profession. If we are not then more than conquerors we are failing as Christians.

(c) The encouragement of history

Now, what is it that makes this possible? The prophet finds his consolation in a right and Christian interpretation of history, to which reference has earlier been made. Whenever, in the Psalms, the writer faces situations such as we are envisaging, he invariably looks back at the history of God's dealings with men and thus finds himself praising God and rejoicing. The prophet likewise here reminds himself of certain of the great facts in the long story of the children of Israel, concentrating especially on the deliverance of Israel from the bondage in Egypt, their passage through the Red Sea, their journey through the wilderness, the defeat of their enemies and their occupation of Canaan.

We too must learn to employ this method. It may be that this will be the only thing that will hold us in the days that lie ahead. As we look out upon the world today is there any cause for rejoicing but this? Whatever may come, if we should ever find ourselves in the fearful state so graphically described by the prophet, the thing to do will be to look back at history.

First, we must *concentrate upon the facts* and realize that they are facts. The prophet goes into great detail in telling us of the things that God had done—how He had divided the Red Sea, halted the sun, and controlled the very elements. There is no question that the facts of the biblical record need to be emphasized above everything else in these days. There are those who tell us that what is needed is a return to biblical theology and a new understanding of the teaching of the Bible. They talk a great deal about the wonderful re-discovery in recent years of the essential message of the Bible. This is the emphasis of what is known as the 'Neo-orthodoxy'. Most of them use the term ' myth ' to describe many of the historical facts, and they say that the actual history is really not important in itself. The events recorded do not ultimately matter. What matters is the *teaching* that is enshrined in the supposed facts. They suggest that the historical details of the Old Testament are not of the first importance, and that it is not really essential for you to believe the facts. What is important is to believe the message which is presented in that form. Hence, many of them do not believe that the children of Israel did literally walk through the Red Sea. They say that it is scientifically impossible. However, they agree that there is an important principle enshrined in the story, and the main thing is to understand that principle. The current term ' myth ' implies that the ' shell ' of history is unimportant; it is the ' kernel ' of truth that matters. The actual facts presented may not be true in themselves but what they represent is true.

Now if that view is true I have no consolation at all. If God did not actually do the things recorded in the Old Testament for Israel, then the whole Bible may be just a piece of psychology meant to keep me happy. The Bible, however, plainly shows that my comfort and consolation lie in facts—the fact that God has done certain things and that they have literally happened. The God in whom I believe is the God who could and *did* divide the Red Sea and the river Jordan. In reminding himself and us of these things, Habakkuk is not just comforting himself by playing with ideas; he is speaking of the things that God has *actually done.* The Christian faith is solidly based upon facts, not ideas. And if the facts recorded in the Bible are not true, then I have no hope and no comfort. For we are not saved by ideas; but by facts, by events. The Christian faith differs from all other religions in that its doctrines are based upon facts. Buddhism, Hinduism and other faiths rest upon theories and ideas. In the Christian faith alone we are dealing with facts. We must reject as from the devil this modern theory about ' myth '.

The facts believed and accepted as such by our Lord are absolutely essential.

Having established the facts, we must reckon on *the greatness of God's power*. The prophet reminds himself of the miracles that God worked in Egypt: ' His brightness was as the light; he had horns coming out of his hand: and there was the hiding of his power. Before him went the pestilence ' (verses 4, 5). Then he speaks of the dividing of the Red Sea: ' Was the Lord displeased against the rivers? was thine anger against the rivers? was thy wrath against the sea, that thou didst ride upon thine horses and thy chariots of salvation? ' (verse 8). It is important to accept the fact that Pharaoh and his hosts were literally drowned in the sea. The story is not a mere allegory of deliverance but an event that actually happened and by which God displayed His power.

There follow references to Mount Sinai, to the dividing of the waters of Jordan, and then there is that striking phrase, ' The sun and moon stood still in their habitation ' (verse 11). God arrested the sun in order that the children of Israel might triumph. The God in whom we believe can act, and does act, how and when it pleases Him. Habakkuk is meditating upon the greatness and the power of God and the miraculous element in God's dealing with His people. If the substance of these miracles is not true, where is our comfort and consolation? The facts are important because they reveal the greatness and the power of God, and the miraculous element in God's dealing with His people.

The third truth is that the God with whom we have to do is *a God who is true to His word and keeps His promises*. ' Thy bow was made quite naked, according to the oaths of the tribes, even thy word. Thou didst cleave the earth with rivers ' (verse 9). The prophet, in reminding himself of the facts and of the power of God, is also assuring himself that, in these events, God was but keeping His word and fulfilling the oath given to Abraham, and repeated to Isaac and Jacob. God had said they were His people and that He had certain purposes for them, and so, though they seemed to be overwhelmed in Egypt, He brought them out and sustained them in all their troubles.

We now see clearly the divinely provided way to deal with the fear which we cannot control ourselves. We look back and think about God. When the prophet did this, he began to feel better. He forgot his nerves and, in contemplation of the mighty, miracle-working God, he was so filled with wonder that he began to rejoice. He then felt he could face whatever might come. In spite of everything he could rejoice in the Lord, and joy in the God of his salvation. Such a God, he knew, would not forget him, and such a God would certainly bring him through.

III. GOD'S MULTIPLIED PROVISION FOR HIS FEARFUL CHURCH

These are the facts which the prophet Habakkuk remembered for his own consolation. But we today are in a still more wonderful position than Habakkuk. We can add to the history, we can supplement the facts adduced by the prophet. We are in a position to see how everything that God revealed to him was literally fulfilled. The Chaldeans were indeed raised up; they did destroy the Israelites; the Israelites were carried away captive into Babylon. But, in due time, God turned upon the Chaldeans and destroyed them, and brought back the remnant of Israel to Jerusalem. The city was re-established and the temple was rebuilt.

We can go further. We can look at the facts of the mighty salvation that God has worked out in Christ. We may rejoice especially in the fact of the Resurrection. If ever a situation seemed absolutely hopeless it was when the Son of God was crucified on a tree and buried in a grave. The disciples were dejected, for indeed the end seemed to have come. But God acted in the miracle of the Resurrection. He showed that He was still God and that, with Him, nothing was impossible. The Resurrection of Jesus Christ is not an idea; but a literal, historical fact. If it is not, there is no gospel. We do not believe merely in some persistence of life beyond the grave. We do not merely say that Jesus still lives. We declare that He literally rose from the grave in the body. Everything depends on the truth of this.

Consider some further facts. The Jews persecuted God's people cruelly, and were warned that if they persisted in so doing they would be finally destroyed. They had been warned in the Old Testament; they were warned again by John the Baptist and by Christ Himself. When they persisted in wrong-doing, God destroyed their city in A.D. 70. The temple was cast down and the people were scattered among the nations, where they still remain. The events of A.D. 70 must never be forgotten. Never forget, either, what happened to the Roman Empire which persecuted the Christian Church and tried to destroy her. But it had been clearly revealed in the Book of Revelation and elsewhere that terrible disaster would overwhelm them and that they would be destroyed. It literally happened as anyone may read in the history of the Roman Empire. These events could be supplemented by many others down the centuries. The story of the Christian Church in the Middle Ages, the story of the Protestant Reformation and the persecution of the

Protestant Fathers illustrate the same principle. The devil, acting through the Roman church, tried to destroy the Protestants and for a time all seemed lost; but onward went the work of God. In the great stories of the Covenanters and of the Puritans are found further illustrations of the same great principle. By reviewing these things we, like Habakkuk, will be able to rejoice in the Lord in spite of circumstances.

Over and above all other facts is the most glorious fact of all, the fact of Jesus Christ Himself. We are given the details of His earthly life in the Gospels so that we may have consolation in times of trouble. Above all remember that the Son of God Himself has been through this world. He knows all about the contradiction of sinners against Himself. Though He was the Son of God He knew what it was to be tired, to be weary, to be faint in His body, to sweat drops of blood in agony. He knew what it was to face the whole world and all the power of Satan and hell massed against Himself. 'We have not an high priest which cannot be touched with the feeling of our infirmities; but was in all points tempted like as we are, yet without sin' (Heb. iv. 15). He knows all about our weakness and our frailty. The incarnation is not a mere idea but a fact: 'The Word was made flesh'. And in our agony and weakness we can always turn to Him with confidence knowing that He understands, He knows, and He can succour. The Son of God became man in order that He might be our perfect High Priest and be able to lead us to God.

> My hope is built on nothing less
> Than Jesu's blood and righteousness.
> I dare not trust my sweetest frame
> But wholly lean on Jesu's Name.

When darkness seems to veil His face
I rest on His unchanging grace;
In every high and stormy gale
My anchor holds within the veil.

His oath, His covenant and blood
Support me in the 'whelming flood.
When all around my soul gives way
He then is all my hope and stay.
    On Christ the solid Rock I stand.
    All other ground is sinking sand.

So, come what may, ' I will rejoice in the Lord, I
will joy in the God of my salvation '.